CAN I BUY
A SLICE
OF SKY?

Poems from Black, Asian
and American Indian cultures

CAN I BUY A SLICE OF SKY?

Poems from Black, Asian and American Indian cultures

Edited by Grace Nichols

Illustrated by Liz Thomas

Hodder
Children's
Books

a division of Hodder Headline Limited

Copyright © 1991 Grace Nichols in this collection

Illustrations © 1991 Liz Thomas

Cover illustration by Mark Miller

First published in Great Britain in 1991 by Blackie and Son Ltd

Knight Books edition 1993

This edition published by Hodder Children's Books 1996

Hodder Children's Books
A Division of Hodder Headline Limited
338 Euston Road
London NW1 3BH

10

British Library C.I.P.

A CIP catalogue record for this title is available
from the British Library

Printed and bound in Great Britain by
Clays Ltd, St Ives plc

ISBN 0 340 58828 4

Contents

* Denotes young Black and Asian poets who were either born in the UK or came to the UK when they were very young.

My Kind of School

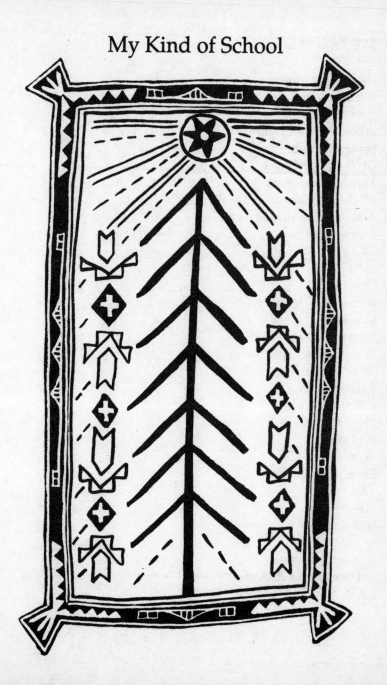

My Kind of School

Deep in the forest
Where a cool breeze
Fans my face,
Where the warm sun
Shines in bright
Geometry problems
Through the leaves
While birds lecture and scold
And squirrels play at recess
Through the trees —
This is my kind of school.

Or give me
A great rock ledge
Overlooking a valley.
Below me, let me study
People as they rush about
As if today stands alone —
Their only time
For running past
Their neighbours.
And still I sit
in quietness,
Learning from them
That to run
Is to run,
Is to run...

RAYMOND TEESETESKIE
American Indian (Cherokee)

Daydreamer

'Aljenard, Winston, Frederick,
Spencer, wha ya look out the winda sa?'
'Me alook pun the nice green grass!'
'But why do you look apun the nice green grass?'
'Me na no!'

'Aljenard, Winston, Frederick Spencer,
wha are ya look out the winda sa?'
'Me alook pun the bright blue sky!'
'But why do you look apun the bright blue sky?'
'Me na no!'

'Aljenard, Winston, Frederick,
Spencer, what are ya look out the winda sa?'
'Me alook pun the hummin burd!'
'But why do you look apun the hummin burd?'
'Me na no!'

'Aljenard, Winston, Frederick,
Spencer, what are you look out the winda sa?'
'Me alook apun the glistening sun!'
'But why you look apun the glistening sun?'
'Me na no!'

'Aljenard, Winston, Frederick,
Spencer, wha are you look out the winda sa?'
'Me a try to feel the nice warm eir!'
'But why do you try to feel the nice warm eir?'

'Cause me a daydreamer!'

DAVID DURHAM
UK*

What The Teacher Said When Asked:
What Er We Avin For Geography Miss?

This morning I've got too much energy
much too much for geography

I'm in a high mood
so class don't think me crude
but you can stuff latitude and longitude

I've had enough of the earth's crust
today I want to touch the clouds

Today I want to sing out loud
and tear all maps to shreds

I'm not settling for river beds
I want the sky and nothing less

Today I couldn't care if east turns west
Today I've got so much energy
I could do press-ups on the desk
but that won't take much out of me

Today I'll dance on the globe
in a rainbow robe

while you class remain seated
on your natural zone
with your pens and things
watching my contours grow wings

All right class, see you later.
If the headmaster asks for me
say I'm a million dreaming degrees
beyond the equator

a million dreaming degrees
beyond the equator

JOHN AGARD
Guyana/UK

Fun

The pedal on our school piano squeaks
And one day Miss Allen stopped playing
And we stopped singing
And Mr Cobb came with the skinny silver can
And gave it a long greasy drink
And the next day when we got ready to sing
Miss Allen smiles
  and blinked her eyes
  and plinked the piano
  and pushed the pedal
And the pedal said
  SQUEEEEEEEAK!
And we laughed
But Miss Allen didn't.

ELOÏSE GREENFIELD
Afro-American

Eleven Years Old

I'm old enough
to work in the fields,
my grandmother says:
your limbs are young
and strong,
your mind won't rust,
we need the extra hands
to tend the crop
and feed the goats
and till this ungrateful land.

Maybe
I'll go to school
when the crop is in,
when we take the few yams
from the soil,
then I'll wear a new dress,
and leave when it's early day,
for it's only one mile to the school.

DIONNE BRAND
Trinidad

Hopscotch

A hip hop hippity hop
yes it's time to play hopscotch
hip hop hippity hop
yes it's time to play hopscotch

a turn and a twist
we make a double fist
a jump and a spin
we go right in

a flop and a hop
I spin like a top
Jessie now stands upside down
her smile looks just like a frown

14

Hey!
a hip hop hippity hop
me and my friends play hopscotch
jumping
   laughing
      running
screaming
hip
   hop
      hippity
hop

we are all having fun
wanting to play till the day is done
until Gloria the big bully
comes and yells

BOYS DON'T PLAY HOPSCOTCH!!!

AFUA COOPER
Jamaica

I Know the Answer

Sir – Sir
I've got my hand up sir
I know the answer,
But once again the teacher
ignores my urgent plea,
That the answer to that question
Has got to be – minus three.

Sir I know the answer
His eyes glance above my head
Instead it's Tommy Tucker
who answers it instead

Who was the first man on the moon?
Me Sir! Me Sir! I know! I know!
SIT QUIET BOY!
Stop jumping about...
There is no need to shout
'The question Mark, is not referred to you...
Can you give me the answer Sue?
Clever girl – that is correct
NOW –
Who knows where the highest mountain in the world is?'

Huh!
if he thinks I'm putting up my hand
he can get lost.
I won't give him the satisfaction
of telling me to sit down –
OK Mark – what's the answer?

Mark! – wake up Mark!
'In which country is the highest mountain?'
Me Sir? Do you mean me Sir?
eh! eh!
I don't know Sir.

P. OMOBOYE
UK*

Confusion

Jean get licks in school today
For hitting Janet Hill
It was just after recess time
And class was playful still
Janet pull Jean ribbon off
And throw it on the ground
Jean got vex and cuff Janet
Same time Miss turn round
Miss didn't ask no questions
She just start beating Jean
Tomorrow Jean mother coming
To fix-up Miss McLean

ODETTE THOMAS
Trinidad

I wish I were ...

When the gong sounds ten in the morning and I
    walk to school by our lane,
Every day I meet the hawker crying, 'Bangles, crystal
    bangles?'
There is nothing to hurry him on, there is no road he
    must take, no place he must go to, no time when he
    must come home.
I wish I were a hawker, spending my day in the road,
    crying 'Bangles, crystal bangles!'
When at four in the afternoon I come back from the
    school,
I can see through the gate of that house the gardener
    digging the ground.
He does what he likes with his spade, he soils his clothes
    with dust,
Nobody takes him to task if he gets baked in the sun or
    gets wet.
I wish I were a gardener digging away at the garden
    with nobody to stop me from digging.

Just as it gets dark in the evening and my mother sends
   me to bed,
I can see through the open window the watchman
   walking up and down.
The lane is dark and lonely, and the street-lamp stands
Like a giant with one red eye in its head.
The watchman swings his lantern and walks with his
   shadow at his side, and never once goes to bed in his
   life.
I wish I were a watchman walking the streets all night,
   chasing the shadows with my lantern.

RABINDRANATH TAGORE
India

two friends

lydia and shirley have
two pierced ears and
two bare ones
five pigtails
two pairs of sneakers
two berets
two smiles
one necklace
one bracelet
lots of stripes and
one good friendship

NIKKI GIOVANNI
Afro-American

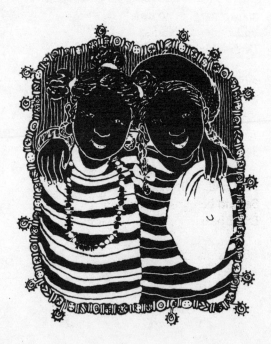

Morning Break

Girls in white blouses, blue skirts,
boys in blue trousers, white shirts,
singing, swinging, screeching, reaching,
hooking wasps, riddle-saying,
ringplaying –
Bayhanna, bayhanna, bayhanna, bay.
If your teachers scold you
Listen to what they say.
That's the way you bayhanna, bayhanna, bay.

Lamppost schoolmaster in grey jacket,
grey tale of wild Abaco hog and donkey;
mild worry, calm hurry,
stiff bones and cane;
ringplaying –
Round the green apple tree
Where the grass grows so sweet,
Miss Della*, Miss Della,
Your true lover was here,
And he wrote you a letter
To turn 'round your head.

First bell, all frozen.
Second bell, instant motion.
Disappear.

TELCINE TURNER
Bahamas

* Or any two-syllabic first name

Miss Pinn

Miss
Pinn
was
tall
and
slim

Whenever she called us
it was like being in a new class –
beyond us.

LESLEY MIRANDA
UK*

No More Latin No More French

No more Latin
No more French
No more sitting
On de old school bench

No more licks
To make me cry
No more eye-water
To come out me eye.

TRADITIONAL
Guyana

When

on a schoolday
I wake to
see
clouds of sky
full of water
I cross my
fingers
RIGHT AWAY
and pray
for the sun
to
PLEASE stay
AWAY and let
it rain
today,
with no big-
people around
to shout
'boy get inside
before you get
wet'
When on a school
day, I like
rain
best,
So come on
cloud unload
your water
fillup the
gutter, nothing
I like better

than Splishing
and Splashing
in rainy weather
  TO
make boats from
big leaves
match-sticks
old boards
and pieces of
wood
put them in the
water and watch
them run
under bridges
round corners
throwing bricks
to make them
spin 'roun
no matter if
they go down
plenty more
where they come
from
  SO
come on cloud
unload, fill the
gutter, if it
floods so much
the better, we'll
turn an ole car
roof over

captain and crew
poling down the
avenue river,
COME ON cloud
DON'T let me
down, let the
rain borrow
today from the
sun, let it tumble
down, just for fun
PLEASE

MARC MATTHEWS
Guyana

A Toast for Everybody Who is Growin

Somebody who is growin
is a girl or a boy –
I tell yu is a girl or a boy –
with hips gettn broader
than a lickle skirt
and shoulders gettn bigger
than a lickle shirt,
wanting six teachers
through the misery of maths
and one – only one –
who never ever get cross.
O, the coconut –
it come from so far
yu think it would-a get
hello, from a hazelnut.

Somebody who is growin
is a girl or a boy –
I tell yu is a girl or a boy –
who ride a bus to school
like an empty pocket fool
yet really well wantin
own, own-a, BMW
to cruise up West and North
and all aroun SW.
O, the pineapple –
it come from so far
yu think it would-a get
hello, from a apple.

Somebody who is growin
is a girl or a boy –
I tell yu is a girl or a boy –
who will never get rich
from a no-inflation boom,
will share no Dallas banquet
that come in own sitting-room,
to keep a bodypopper
with a crummy-crummy supper.
O, yu think it would-a mek
a stone scream
rollin down a hill
jumpin in-a stream.
But, in spite of everythin,
everybody who's growin
GO ON, nah! GO ON. Just do that thing.

JAMES BERRY
Jamaica/UK

The Big Open

Hurricane

Shut the windows
Bolt the doors
Big rain coming
Climbing up the mountain

Neighbours whisper
Dark clouds gather
Big rain coming
Climbing up the mountain

Gather in the clothes lines
Pull down the blinds
Big wind rising
Coming up the mountain

Branches falling
Raindrops flying
Tree tops swaying
People running
Big wind blowing
Hurricane! on the mountain.

DIONNE BRAND
Trinidad

I Wonder

I wonder
who lives
in the sky
way up high
above the clouds

I wonder
what they have
for lunch
and what their
house looks like

I truly wonder
who lives in the sky
way above the clouds
into the endless blue space
beyond which I cannot see

I know someone
lives up there
because sometimes
just like me
she gets very sad
and tears fall
from her eyes
on top of my roof
on my grass
on my plants
on my head
if I go outside

I wonder
what makes her sad
and why she cries
this rain that
comes from the sky.

OPAL PALMER ADISA
Jamaica

First Song of the Thunder

Thonah! Thonah!
There is a voice above,
The voice of the thunder.
Within the dark cloud,
Again and again it sounds,
Thonah! Thonah!

Thonah! Thonah!
There is a voice below,
The voice of the grasshopper.
Among the plants,
Again and again it sounds,
Thonah! Thonah!

American Indian (Navaho)
Translated by Dr Washington Matthews

Rain

Today the rain
is an aged man
a grey old man
a curious old man
in a music store

Today houses
are strings of a harp
soprano harp strings
bass harp strings
in a music store

The ancient man
strums the harp
with thin long fingers
attentively picking
a weary jingle
a soft jazzy jangle
then dodders away
before the boss comes 'round...

FRANK MARSHALL DAVIS
Afro-American

Sun and Shade

Sun you are beautiful, oh beautiful,
you give us warm sunshine,
we love you so much, oh sunshine.
Shade you clumsy nonsense go away,
nobody loves you,
everybody hates you.

Shade you are beautiful, oh beautiful –
and cool.
We love you so much.
Sunshine you clumsy nonsense go away,
Nobody loves you,
everybody hates you,
shade cool shade, oh come.

MICHAEL MONDO
Papua New Guinea (Chimbu)

The Picnic in Jammu

Uncle Ayub swung me round and round
till the horizon became a rail
banked high upon the Himalayas.
The trees signalled me past. I whistled,
shut my eyes through tunnels of the air.
The family laughed, watching me puff
out my muscles, healthily aggressive.

This was late summer, before the snows
come to Kashmir, this was picnic time.

Then, uncoupling me from the sky, he
plunged me into the river, himself
a bough with me dangling at its end.
I went purple as a plum. He reared
back and lowered the branch of his arm
to grandma who swallowed me with a kiss.
Laughter peeled away my goosepimples.

This was late summer, before the snows
come to Kashmir, this was picnic time.

After we'd eaten, he aimed grapes at
my mouth. I flung at him the shells of
pomegranates and ran off. He tracked
me down the river-bank. We battled,
melon-rind and apple-core our arms.
'You two!' grandma cried. 'Stop fighting, you'll
tire yourselves to death!' We didn't listen.

This was late summer, before the snows
come to Kashmir and end children's games.

ZULFIKAR GHOSE
Pakistan

Fisherman Chant

Sister river
Brother river
Mother river
Father river
O life giver
O life taker
O friend river
What have you
in store
for a poor
fisherman
today?

From my boat
I cast my net
to your heart
O friend river
and I hope

you return it
gleaming with silver
O friend river

Sister river
Brother river
Mother river
Father river
O life giver
O life taker
O friend river
What have you
in store
for a poor fisherman
today?

JOHN AGARD
Guyana/UK

Morning

Day came in
on an old brown bus
with two friends.
She crept down
an empty street
bending over
to sweep the thin dawn away.
With her broom,
she drew red streaks
in the corners
of the dusty sky
and finding a rooster still asleep,
prodded him into song.
A fisherman,
not far from the shore,
lifted his eyes,
saw her coming,
and yawned.
The bus rolled by,
and the two friends caught
a glimpse of blue
as day swung around a corner
to where the sea met a road.
The sky blinked,
woke up,
and might have changed its mind,
but day had come.

DIONNE BRAND
Trinidad

Imagining India

Wide sandy roads with palm trees on either side
and bullocks, buffaloes and peacocks on them.

Some big brick houses
And other little mud ones.

At bazaars
People are buying
And selling
Saris, kurtas,
Herbs and spices.

The setting sun reflecting
on the cool water.

GEETANJALI MOHINI GUPTARA (AGE 9)
UK*

It is Snowing

It is snowing
it is snowing
and the world is white
white
white
snow falls from the sky
in small drops
in big drops
in whole showersful
sometimes it is gentle
and plays with you
it falls softly on your nose
sometimes it falls so hard
you want to cry
Sometimes it becomes a blizzard
a storm
and you cannot go to school
or out to play
you watch the storm from your window
with your nose pressed against it
When the snow settles
you can ski
skate
go tobogganing
or make a snowman or woman

In Spanish snow is la nieve
In Swahili snow is Theluji
and
In French snow is La niege
The Inuit people have 22 different names for snow

AFUA COOPER
Jamaica

They Ran Out of Mud

There is a little hut
Built across from here;
They've mudded two walls
And the rest stands unmade...
For they ran out of mud.

There is a deep gully
Running along the road;
They have filled it halfway
And the rest is still gaping...
For they ran out of mud.

There is a pot by the altar
That they began to mould;
They finished the base
But the rest remains undone...
For they ran out of mud.

Mud! Mud!
Who can find mud?
Maybe if it were gold
Someone would.

MIRIAM KHAMADI
Nigeria

41

Sampan

Waves lap lap
Fish fins clap clap
Brown sails flap flap
Chop-sticks tap tap
Up and down the long green river
Ohe Ohe lanterns quiver
Willow branches brush the river
Ohe Ohe lanterns quiver
Waves lap lap
Fish fins clap clap
Brown sails flap flap
Chop-sticks tap tap

TAO LANG PEE
China

42

The Kangaroo

Water beneath the hills,
running slowly from the creek,
towards the hills.

Birds sitting on the branch,
smelling the red flowers
that are growing.

Kangaroo is lying in the shade,
very tired from hopping around,
he listens to the water,
that is running very slowly.

He is happy, no people around,
to spear him.
He smells the red flowers,
so tired he goes to sleep.

PANSY ROSE NAPALJARRI
Aboriginal/Australia

Banyan tree

Moonshine tonight, come mek we dance and sing,
Moonshine tonight, come mek we dance and sing,
Me deh rock so, yu deh rock so, under banyan tree,
Me deh rock so, yu deh rock so, under banyan tree.

Ladies mek curtsy, an gentlemen mek bow,
Ladies mek curtsy, an gentlemen mek bow,
Me deh rock so, yu deh rock so, under banyan tree,
Me deh rock so, yu deh rock so, under banyan tree.
Den we join hans an dance around an roun,
Den we join hans an dance around an roun,
Me deh rock so, yu deh rock so, under banyan tree,
Me deh rock so, yu deh rock so, under banyan tree.

TRADITIONAL
Jamaica

Heart of the Woods

Deep into the woods we'll go,
Hand in hand.
Let the woods close about us,
Let the world outside be lost –
And let us find that Secret City
Lost so long ago –
In the Heart of the Woods.

WESLEY CURTRIGHT
Afro-American

Love and Praises

Honey I Love

I love
I love a lot of things, a whole lot of things
Like
My cousin comes to visit and you know he's from the South
'Cause every word he says just kind of slides out of his mouth
I like the way he whistles and I like the way he walks
But honey, let me tell you that I LOVE the way he talks
   I love the way my cousin talks

                and

The day is hot and icky and the sun sticks to my skin
Mr Davis turns the hose on, everybody jumps right in
The water stings my stomach and I feel so nice and cool
Honey let me tell you that I LOVE a flying pool
   I love to feel a flying pool

                and

Renee comes out to play and brings her doll without a dress
I make a dress with paper and that doll sure looks a mess
We laugh so loud and long and hard the doll falls to the
   ground
Honey, let me tell you that I LOVE the laughing sound
   I love to make the laughing sound

                and

My uncle's car is crowded and there's a lot of food to eat
We're going down the country where the church folks like to
    meet
I'm looking out the window at the cows and trees outside
Honey, let me tell you that I LOVE to take a ride
    I just love to take a family ride
                          and

My mama's on the sofa sewing buttons on my coat
I go and sit beside her, I'm through playing with my boat
I hold her arm and kiss it, 'cause it feels so soft and warm
Honey, let me tell you that I LOVE my mama's arm
    I love to kiss my mama's arm
                          and

It's not so late at night, but still I'm lying in my bed
I guess I need my rest, at least that's what my mama said
She told me not to cry 'cause she don't want to hear a peep
Honey, let me tell you I DONT love to go to sleep
    I do not love to go to sleep

But I love
I love a lot of things, a whole lot of things
And honey,
I love you, too.

ELOISE GREENFIELD
Afro-American

The Older the Violin the Sweeter the Tune

Me Granny old
Me Granny wise
stories shine like a moon
from inside she eyes.

Me Granny can dance
Me Granny can sing
but she can't play violin.

Yet she always saying,
'Dih older dih violin
de sweeter de tune.'

Me Granny must be wiser
than the man inside the moon.

JOHN AGARD
Guyana/UK

A Black Love-Song

Seen my lady home last night
    Jump back, honey, jump back.
Held her hand and squeezed it tight,
    Jump back, honey, jump back.
Heard her sigh a little sigh,
Seen a light gleam from her eye
And a smile go flitting by –
    Jump back, honey, jump back.

Heard de wind blow through de pine,
    Jump back, honey, jump back.
Mockingbird was singing fine
    Jump back, honey, jump back.
And my heart was beating so
When I reached my lady's do'
Dat I couldn't bear to go –
    Jump back, honey, jump back.

Put my arm around her waist,
    Jump back, honey, jump back.
Raised her lips and took a taste
    Jump back, honey, jump back.
Love me, honey, love me true?
Love me well as I love you?
And she answered, 'Course I do' –
    Jump back, honey, jump back.

PAUL LAURENCE DUNBAR
Afro-American

Poem in the Post

A glance at the bought postcard
and glib phrases reappear:
"having a wonderful time...
sun 'n sand... wish you were here...
love..."
No, I will not send to you
postcards for acquaintances
to be treated to envied
suntanned holiday instances.
Love,
I shall send you a vision
of our future together,
I shall post you a poem:
crystallised perfume of rare
love.

DEBJANI CHATTERJEE
India

My Baby Has No Name Yet

My baby has no name yet;
like a new-born chick or puppy,
my baby is not named yet.

What numberless texts I examined
at dawn and night and evening over again!
But not one character did I find
which is as lovely as the child.
Starry field of the sky,
or heap of pearls in the depth.
Where can the name be found, how can I?

My baby has no name yet;
like an unnamed bluebird or white flowers
from the farthest land for the first,
I have no name for this baby of ours.

KIM NAM-JO
Korea
Translated by Ko Won

Ballad of Birmingham

'Mother dear, may I go downtown
instead of out to play,
and march the streets of Birmingham
in a freedom march today?'

'No, baby, no, you may not go,
for the dogs are fierce and wild,
and clubs and hoses, guns and jails
ain't good for a little child.'

'But, mother, I won't be alone.
Other children will go with me,
and march the streets of Birmingham
to make our country free.'

'No, baby, no, you may not go,
for I fear those guns will fire.
But you may go to church instead,
and sing in the children's choir.'

She has combed and brushed her nightdark hair,
and bathed rose-petal sweet,
and drawn white gloves on her small brown hands,
and white shoes on her feet.

The mother smiled to know her child
was in the sacred place,
but that smile was the last smile
to come upon her face.

For when she heard the explosion,
her eyes grew wet and wild.
She raced through the streets of Birmingham
calling for her child.

She clawed through bits of glass and brick,
then lifted out a shoe.
'O, here's the shoe my baby wore,
but, baby, where are you?'

DUDLEY RANDALL
Afro-American

Teasing Song

A: Hey, young bride!
    Let us go and draw water!

B: I'm not going. I'm ill.

> Little crooked-flower, gwenxe, gwenxe!
> Little crooked-legs, gwenxe, gwenxe!

A: Hey, young bride,
    Let us go and gather firewood!

B: I'm not going. I'm ill.

> Little crooked-flower, gwenxe, gwenxe!
> Little crooked-legs, gwenxe, gwenxe!

A: Hey, young bride,
    You are being called to the bridal bed!

B: I'm coming. I feel a bit better now!

> Little crooked-flower, gwenxe, gwenxe!
> Little crooked-legs, gwenxe, gwenxe!

PRINCESS MAGOGO
Zulu

Under the Mistletoe

I did not know she'd take it so,
   Or else I'd never dared;
Although the bliss was worth the blow,
I did not know she'd take it so.
She stood beneath the mistletoe
So long I thought she cared;
I did not know she'd take it so,
Or else I'd never dared.

COUNTEE CULLEN
Afro-American

Sea Lyric

Over the seas tonight, love
   Over the darksome deeps,
Over the seas tonight, love
   Slowly my vessel creeps.

Over the seas tonight, love,
   Walking the sleeping foam –
Sailing away from thee love,
   Sailing from thee and home.

Over the seas tonight, love,
   Dreaming beneath the spars –
Till in my dreams you shine, love,
   Bright as the listening stars.

WILLIAM STANLEY BRAITHWAITE
Afro-American

In Praise of Noses

Not exactly ornamental
even when quite straight,
these funny, two-holed things!

But think:
if they faced upwards
they'd blow hats off

when one sneezed
and fill with rain
when it poured.

If sideways,
what objects of derision
snuff-takers would be!

Now all that a sneeze merits
is a 'God bless'.

God bless indeed, sweet nose,
warming, filtering,

humidifying the air as I breathe,
you do a marvellous job!

PRABHU S. GUPTARA
India/UK

Steelband Jump Up

I put my ear to the ground,
And I hear the steelband sound:
Ping pong! Ping pong!
Music deep, rhythm sweet,
I'm dancing tracking the beat;
Like a sea-shell's ringing song,
Ping pong! Ping pong!
Moving along, moving along,
High and low, up and down,
Ping pong! Ping pong!
Pan beating singing, round and round,
Ping pong! Ping pong!

FAUSTIN CHARLES
Trinidad

The Literary Cat

Dedicated to my Great Aunt Marie

A fire, peace and a book; all a cat wants.
The book's most important.

When humans don't watch and cats are warm,
Spectacles worn,
open slides the bookcase –
secret.
The Marvellous Adventures of Pussykins
is drawn from the shelf.
Happy now,
purring,
our hero puss not stirring,
purr, purr, purr.

RANJEET MOHAN GUPTARA (AGED 10)
UK

To You, Ant

Ant, who gave you your unique skill
To pile up soil in that weird conical mount at your doorstep
So that when it rains the water will be run off without
   getting into your house?
Ant, my friend, you are a genius.

I envy your strength, Ant.
Bees and crickets are no match for you in a fight;
And with a long stick you even strike away at scorpions,
You have never been beaten in a fight.

Ant, where from do you get your daring?
You enter an elephant's trunk and it throws itself about in pain;
You attack and smother to death a giant python;
And you can even crawl on the chin of a sleeping crocodile.

Where from does your strength come, Ant?
You dig a hole that never bends;
You hollow your way through the trunks of trees
Digging deeper passing on down beyond the roots.

Ant, you are the pillar of your house.
At the birth of your child
You go to hunt for food in deep dark forests,
Ant, your ways will never cease to surprise me.

Ant, you are indeed a great hunter;
You never fail to give your children food;
You care for the nursing mothers with loving gentleness.
No one ever goes hungry in your household.

Tell me Ant, where did you get this love?
There is no jealousy nor stinting in your city.
You work all day long without complaining or grumbling.
Please lend me your heart for just one day.

Ant, why is it that you never seem to grow old?
Unless someone steps on you and kills you, I haven't seen your
    corpse anywhere.
Please give me your knowledge of life
So that I can help my children and friends.

Southern Africa (Shona)
Translated by the Literature Bureau

Song of the Horse

How joyous his neigh!
Lo, the Turquoise Horse of Johano-Ai,
    How joyous his neigh!
There on precious hides outspread standeth he;
    How joyous his neigh.
There on tips of fair fresh flowers feedeth he;
    How joyous his neigh.
There of mingled waters holy drinketh he;
    How joyous his neigh.
There he spurneth dust of glittering grains;
    How joyous his neigh.
There in mist of sacred pollen hidden, all hidden he;
    How joyous his neigh.
There his offspring may grow and thrive for evermore;
    How joyous his neigh!

American Indian (Navaho)
Translated by Curtis (Burlin) Natalie

April Rain Song

Let the rain kiss you.
Let the rain beat upon your head with silver
    liquid drops.
Let the rain sing you a lullaby.

The rain makes still pools on the side walk.
The rain makes running pools in the gutter.
The rain plays a little sleep-song on our roof at night –

And I love the rain.

LANGSTON HUGHES
Afro-American

Night in the Lap of Morning

Night so smooth
night so deep
night in the lap of morning
night in the arms of another night

Sky dog black as night
come let me hold you tight

Night so smooth
night so deep
night in the lap of morning
night in the arms of another night

Moon tiger
when you leap
stars start their falling

Night so smooth
night so deep
night in the lap of morning
night in the arms of another night

African bird
fly home to me
fly across the deep blue sea

Night so smooth
night so deep
night in the lap of morning
night in the arms of another night

Caw crow
caw up a moonbow

Night so smooth
night so deep
night in the lap of morning
night in the arms of another night

Midnight caterpillar
keep crawling
birds have gone to sleep

Night so smooth
night so deep
night in the lap of morning
night in the arms of another night

SUNDAIRA MORNINGHOUSE
Afro-American

Rain O, rain O!

Rain o, rain o!
Return to the hills,
Grandmother is trying to come home.

HARRIVAKORE MARIPO (OROKOLO)
Papua New Guinea

The Reason I Like Chocolate

The Reason I Like Chocolate

The reason I like chocolate
is I can lick my fingers
and nobody tells me I'm not polite

I especially like scary movies
'cause I can snuggle with Mommy
or my big sister and they don't laugh

I like to cry sometimes 'cause
everybody says 'what's the matter
don't cry'

and I like books
for all those reasons
but mostly 'cause they just make me
happy

and I really like
to be happy

NIKKI GIOVANNI
Afro-American

Dumplins

'Janey, you see nobody pass here?'
  'No me friend.'
'Sarah, you see nobody pass here?'
  'No me friend.'
'Well, one of me dumplins gone.'
  'Don't tell me so!'
'One of me dumplins gone.'
'Janey, you see nobody pass here?'
  'No, me friend.'
'Sarah, you see nobody pass here?'
  'No, me friend.'
'Well, two of me dumplins gone.'
  'Don't tell me so!'
'Two of me dumplins gone.'

TRADITIONAL
Caribbean

The Lychee

Fruit white and lustrous as a pearl...
Lambent as the jewel of Ho, more strange
Than the saffron-stone of Hsia.
Now sigh we at the beauty of its show,
Now triumph in its taste.
Sweet juices lie in the mouth,
Soft scents invade the mind.
All flavours here are joined, yet none is master;
A hundred diverse tastes
Blend in such harmony no man can say
That one outstrips the rest. Sovereign of sweets,
Peerless, pre-eminent fruit, who dwellest apart
In noble solitude!

WANG I
China
Translated by Arthur Waley

End

Once upon a time,
    Goose drank wine,
Monkey chewed tobacco
    On the streetcar line.
Streetcar broke,
    Monkey choke,
And that was the end
    Of the monkey joke.

TRADITIONAL
Afro-American

Fruits

Half a paw-paw in the basket
Only one o we can have it,
Wonder which one that will be?
I have a feeling that is me.

One guinep up in the tree
Hanging down there tempting me,
It don' mek no sense to pick it,
One guinep can't feed a cricket.

Two ripe guava pon the shelf,
I know I hide them there meself,
When night come an' it get dark
Me an' them will have a talk.

Three sweet-sop, well I just might
give one o' them a nice big bite,
Cover up the bite jus' so, sis,
Then no one will ever notice.

71

Four red apple near me chair,
Who so careless put them there?
Them don' know how me love apple?
Well, thank God fe silly people.

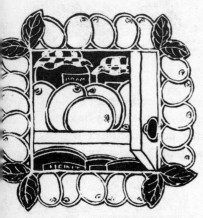

Five jew-plum, I can't believe it!
How they know jew-plum's me fav'rit?
But why they hide them in the cupboard?
Cho, people can be so awkward.

Six naseberry, you want a nibble?
Why baby must always dribble?
Come wipe you mout' it don't mek sense
To broadcast the evidence.

Seven mango! What a find,
The smaddy who lef them really kind,
One fe you and six fe me,
If you want more climb the tree.

72

Eight orange fe Cousin Clem,
but I have just one problem,
How to get rid o' the eight skin
That the orange them come in.

Nine jackfruit! Not even me
can finish nine, but let me see,
I don't suppose that they will miss one?
That was hard but now me done.

Ten banana, mek them stay,
I feeling really full today,
Mek me lie down on me bed, quick,
Lawd, a feeling really sick.

VALERIE BLOOM
Jamaica

Weevilly Porridge

Weevilly porridge I'm going insane
Weevilly porridge gonna wreck my brain
Stir in treacle, make'em taste sweet
Put'em on stove, turn'em up heat
Milk from powder tin, milk from goat
Weevilly porridge, pour'em down throat.

MmmMmm, mission food, send'em from heaben must be good
MmmMmm, mission food, send'em from heaben must be good

Nebba mind the weevil, nebba mind the taste
Missionary she bin say, 'don't you waste'
Weevilly porridge make'em pretty strong
Spread'em on Dampa can't go wrong.

Bless'em little weevil, bless'em little me
We bin lunga trick'em just you see
Catch'em little weevil, put'em in the tea
Only fullah drink'em up Missionary.

Protector He bin call on us give us daily ration
Cook'em plenty food for Him, together we bin mash'em
Weevils in the sago, weevils in the rice
Protector He bin lunga saying - Mmmm, taste nice.

EVA JOHNSON
Aboriginal/Australia

John Belly Grow

Ah was digging potatoes
John Belly grow;
An' ah dig ten basket,
John Belly grow;
No man to pass here,
John Belly grow;
An' the police can't catch me,
John Belly grow;
Right round de harbour,
John Belly grow;
No coo-coo 'pon de table,
John Belly grow.

TRADITIONAL
Jamaica

Kensington Market

Colours
Colours
Colours everywhere
colours of food
   and
colours of people
music sounding
music pounding
Kensington Market on a Saturday morning.

Every Saturday morning
Mom takes her shopping basket
and we go to Kensington Market
Bananas
yams
pumpkin
mangos
okras
and
'whappen'!
Caribbean scent.

Fish with sad eyes
eels
salmon
snapper
and the pretty parrot
Portuguese/Atlantic
Nuts and dried fruits
Mexican herbs and spices
it's Pacos' store
and 'Como estas'.

Chop suey
fried rice
spices from the east
it's Chinese.

The smell of cloves
drifts down the street
it's coming from
the Indonesian restaurant.

All of these mix with music
the sound of
Soca jamming
and
Reggae blasting
'yeah man'!

Colours of food
colours of people
colours of scents
colours of sounds
RED GREEN AND GOLD
Kensington Market on a Saturday morning

AFUA COOPER
Jamaica

Grown-up Blues...Children Blues

Grown-Up Blues

Mother used to come when I was sick,
give me a thermometer to check my fever,
make me swallow orange aspirins,
(the ones for kids)
and tuck me in bed.

Dad used to come when I was sick
feel my forehead,
and ask if my chest hurt,
and tell me to lie down when I already was

Nobody comes now when I'm sick.
I have to feel my own forehead,
take my own temperature,
and swallow two white aspirins,
(the ones for adults).

TERRY KEE
Singapore

The Two Mothers

The two mothers both sit down near the fire at evening
talking about their daughters.
The one is Napangardi and the other is Nangala.

The Nangala started to say a few words about her daughter.
She said, 'My daughter Napaljarri always comes after
midnight from watching videos.
I don't even know where she watches videos, maybe
somewhere in those houses.
Her two eyes don't even hurt and she doesn't even get cramp
from watching the video.'

Then later the other woman Napangardi started to say a few
words about her daughter too.
'Oh no wait till you hear about my daughter Nangala. She
keeps listening to the radio, she listens to the radio from 8.30
in the morning until 7.30 in the night!

'She keeps listening, listening, true. She never stops listening
to the radio. I think I better put a stop to her. I said "when you
listen to the radio so aloud, you will go deaf." That's
what I said to my daughter Nangala.'

RHONDA SAMUEL NAPURRURLA
Aboriginal/Australia

81

A Comb

I am not bald
Not really
Just thin hair
You know

When I went to
Buy
A comb
I thought I saw
The shopkeeper
Grin

No
He didn't smile
But when I left
I felt
There was a horrible
Smirk
On his twisted
Paan chewing
Orange mouth.

GAUTAM VOHRA
Africa

The Clown's Wife

About my husband, the clown,
what could I say?

On stage, he's a different person.
Up there he's a king on a throne,
but at home you should hear him moan.

The moment he walks through that door
without that red nose and them funny clothes,
he seems to have the world on his shoulder.

I do me best to cheer him up, poor soul.
I juggle with eggs, I turn cartwheels,
I tell jokes, I do me latest card trick,
I even have a borrow of his red nose.

But he doesn't say exactly how he feels,
doesn't say what's bothering him inside.
Just sits there saying almost to himself:

'O life, ah life,
what would I do without this clown of a wife?'

JOHN AGARD
Guyana/UK

83

Blaming Sons
(an apology for his own drunkenness)

White hairs cover my temples,
I am wrinkled and gnarled beyond repair,
And though I have five sons,
They all hate paper and brush.
A-shu is eighteen:
For laziness there is none like him.
A-hsuan does his best,
But really loathes the Fine Arts.
Yung and Tuan are thirteen,
But do not know 'six' from 'seven'.
T'ung-tzu in his ninth year
Is only concerned with things to eat.
If Heaven treats me like this,
What can I do but fill my cup?

Chinese
Translated by Arthur Waley

I built my canoe
I worked my garden
O my neck, my neck!
We hunted far in the bush
I built my canoe,
O my bones, my bones!
I burnt the timber
O my back!
I collected bananas,
O my head!
I cut sugarcane
O my back!
I speared some fish
O my hands!

STELLA MIRIA (RORO)
Papua New Guinea

me in the morning

The alarm's just gone
In comes my mum
'Come on young boy it's time to arise'
This is not possible with a ton of sleep in my eyes
Not for me the slothful sliding out of slumber
Nay instead the bombastic bursts of Big Ben's thunder
Oh where's my shoes, oh where's my socks?
Oh who the hell invented clocks?
Oh where's my pants? my brain's awry
Oh God I feel I surely must die
What shirt to wear? which tie will match?
Decisions, decisions oh I think I'll have a scratch
A comb, a comb, my kingdom for a comb
It's gone, it's gone, my comb's left home
Stolen I suppose by some comb-loving gnome
The sheet's warmth comforts my sorrow
I'll go to work but on the morrow

LYNFORD FRENCH
UK

Only the Moon

When I was a child I thought
the new moon was a cradle
The full moon was granny's round face.

The new moon was a banana
The full moon was a big cake.

When I was a child
I never saw the moon
I only saw what I wanted to see.

And now I see the moon
It's the moon
Only the moon, and nothing but the moon.

WONG MAY
Singapore
Translated by E. Thumboo

Chillren, Chillren

Chillren, Chillren,
Yes Mama.

Where you been to?
Grandmama.
What she gave you?
Bread and cheese.

Where is mine?
On de shelf.

How kyan I get it?
Climb on a chair.

Suppose I fall?
I don' care.

What you Mudder an' Fadder
Going eat tonight?

Crappo guts
An' saltfish-tail.

Bad pickney you na care.
Wicked pickney you na care.

ORAL TRADITION
Guyana

For Kalpana

How parents worry
when a child is thin
　　what shall we do
　　what shall we do
they whisper in the night
their voices grey
in the anxieties of love
till the luminous
angel of sleep
leads them softly
(their souls and bodies intertwining)
to her own open city
where they see again
the big bright advertisements
for tonic and vitamins A B C
D E unto infinity.

And they watch their child daily
eating breakfast
greasy egg-yolk egg-white
jams jellies toast and porridge
fat with the milk of human kindness
or dinner
of curry-drowned rice
and momentous salad
　　eat eat my child
　　how thin you are
so the child looks down
distastefully
and eats and eats
but it does no good

while other people's children
grown pink and plump
on fresh air and foolishness.

The cosmos conspires
to keep their child thin
flesh of their flesh
she sings like the wind
she laughs like a river
she sleeps like a flower
but the parents despair
in the bland glare of marriage
and look with narrowed eyes
as though threading a needle
at their tall
thin
perfectly happy
altogether delightful daughter.

NISSIM EZEKIEL
India

91

What To Do?

Don't lean out the window
Or you will fall through
Don't stick out your tongue
It's a rude thing to do

Don't talk with your mouth full
And don't suck your thumb
When you're at the table
Don't sing and don't hum

Don't point
Or throw stones
And don't bite
Don't tell tales
Don't tease
And don't fight

Now after all that
You are lucky if you
Can find even one single thing
You can do!

PAMELA MORDECAI
Jamaica

Granny Granny Please Comb My Hair

Granny Granny
please comb my hair
you always take your time
you always take such care

You put me to sit on a cushion
between your knees
you rub a little coconut oil
parting gentle as a breeze

Mummy Mummy
she's always in a hurry–hurry
rush
she pulls my hair
sometimes she tugs

But Granny
you have all the time in the world
and when you're finished
you always turn my head and say
'Now who's a nice girl.'

GRACE NICHOLS
UK

De More De Merrier

sitting on the
window sill
looking down
on the street
watching folks
go by
wanting
to be there
in the midst
of it all
but stuck up
here all by myself
no friend
no sister
no brother
not even a dog
to talk to

mama off
somewhere
doing chores
papa still
at work
just me
all by myself
warned not to
go anywhere
told not
to let anyone in
not even a friend
especially if

he's a boy

rules
nothing but rules
not allowed
to choose
not allowed
to decide for
myself

i guess
the more the merrier
only applies
to relatives
who come to visit
on holidays

OPAL PALMER ADISA
Jamaica

My Name Is I Don't Know

My name is I Don't Know
I wish it was something else.
I work so hard trying to keep my world clean,
Then along comes some unkind creature
    and drops a litter or two
Then I have to clean it up.

Along comes someone else and does the same,
So I have no sleep.
I wish there was someone else
I would be able to have a nap.

VIVIAN USHERWOOD
*UK**

Boring Chores

On my bedroom door
is a list of chores:
washing, dusting, and all that.

No time to chat –
nothing like that.

Boring, boring chores.

RANJEET MOHAN GUPTARA (AGE 10)
*UK**

Hanging Fire

I am fourteen
and my skin has betrayed me
the boy I cannot live without
still sucks his thumb
in secret
how come my knees are
always so ashy
what if I die
before morning
and momma's in the bedroom
with the door closed.

I have to learn how to dance
in time for the next party
my room is too small for me
suppose I die before graduation
they will sing sad melodies
but finally
tell the truth about me
There is nothing I want to do
and too much
that has to be done
and momma's in the bedroom
with the door closed.

Nobody even stops to think
about my side of it
I should have been on Math Team
my marks were better than his
why do I have to be
the one

wearing braces
I have nothing to wear tomorrow

will I live long enough
to grow up
and momma's in the bedroom
with the door closed.

AUDRE LORDE
Afro-American

People! People! People!

Anancy

Anancy is a trickster of no small order
half a man and half a spider
Miss Muffet was sure glad
he hadn't sat beside her

He's unlike any of your friends
He's a whole lot smarter
he tricks and he outsmarts
He's a real fast talker

He's slow on his feet
a zip on his wit
When it comes to thinking quick
he's a wizard at tricks

He's never lost a game
'cause he cheats, doublecrosses his friends
When he can't win fair
he's a spider again

Anancy is a trickster of no small order
half a man and half a spider
Miss Muffet was sure glad
he hadn't sat beside her

LILLIAN ALLEN
Jamaica

Roots Man
(for Jeremiah Davy)
A Digging Song

Some days I dig de groun... Uh-huh
Some days I plant de lan... Uh-huh
Some days I water de crops... Uh-huh
For I am a roots man... Uh-huh

And when de crops produce... Uh-huh
And when I reap de lan... Uh-huh
I know where de goods come from... Uh-huh
For I put in de roots man... Uh-huh

But when I think 'bout this man... Uh-huh
I don't know where I come from... Uh-huh
Some say I am African... Uh-huh
Some say I am Jamaican... Uh-huh

I want to know where I come from... Uh-huh
Does my life have a future plan?... Uh-huh
I want to know who plant this man... Uh-huh
I want to know my roots man!... Uh-huh

GRACE WALKER GORDON
Jamaica

Mamacita

Mamacita
I love to meet'cha
coming down the street
How was work?
What a pretty skirt!
Did you buy something good to eat?

Mamacita Mamacita
can I stay outside and play?
Oh-yes! Oh-yea!
I will play
on the steps
with Elisha and Kay
And when the sun is almost down
I'll turn around
touch the ground
stamp my feet
jump across the street
and come inside for supper!

SUNDAIRA MORNINGHOUSE
Afro-American

Holding On

I do not know if he was a sage,
nor if he was a philosopher.
I only know that he sat crosslegged,
silent on the sand by the river.

'Tell me the meaning of life,' I begged.
He smiled and answered me not a word.
'I'll not leave empty-handed,' I said.
He smiled and I wondered if he heard.

Exasperated I made to go
when he smiled and gathered me up some sand.
As he turned and looked into my eyes,
he let it trickle from his hand.

Uncertainly I pulled out my purse.
(Had he somehow answered after all?)
Hesitant, I gave a rupee note.
He smiled and slowly let it fall.

DEBJANI CHATTERJEE
India

Old Man Know-All

Old Man Know-All, he comes around
With his nose in the air, turned away from the ground.
His old hair hadn't been combed for weeks.
He said, 'Keep still while Know-All speaks.'

Old Man Know-All's tongue did run.
He knew everything under the sun.
When you knew one thing, he knew more.
He talked enough to make a hearing aid sore.

Old Man Know-All died last week.
He got drowned in the middle of the creek.
The bridge was there and there to stay –
But he knew too much to cross that way.

TRADITIONAL
Afro-American

Timing

Now and then she would shout in church,
Walking down the aisle,
With one hand raised toward heaven
Screaming all the while.

She wanted to be seen
When she was all decked out,
When wearing a new dress or hat
Was the only time she'd shout.

ELMA STUCKEY
Afro-American

My Cousin Melda

My Cousin Melda
she don't make fun
she ain't afraid of anyone
even mosquitoes
when they bite her
she does bite them back
and say –
'Now tell me, how you like that?'

GRACE NICHOLS
Guyana/UK

Water Everywhere

There's water on the ceiling,
And water on the wall,
There's water in the bedroom,
And water in the hall,
There's water on the landing,
And water on the stair,
Whenever Daddy takes a bath
There's water everywhere.

VALERIE BLOOM
Jamaica

107

Sailor

He sat upon the rolling deck
Half a world away from home,
And smoked a Capstan cigarette
And watched the blue waves tipped with foam.

He had a mermaid on his arm,
An anchor on his breast,
And tattooed on his back he had
A blue bird in a nest.

LANGSTON HUGHES
Afro-American

To James

Do you remember
How you won
That last race?
How you flung your body
At the start...
How your spikes
Ripped the cinders
In the stretch...
How you catapulted
Through the tape...
Do you remember?
Don't you think
I lurched with you
Out of those starting holes?
Don't you think
My sinews tightened
At those first
Few strides...
And when you flew into the stretch
Was not all my thrill
Of a thousand races
In your blood?
At your final drive
through the finish line
Did not my shout
Tell of the
Triumphant ecstasy
Of victory?
Live
As I have taught you
To run, Boy —

It's a short dash
Dig your starting holes
Deep and firm
Lurch out of them
Into the straightaway
With all the power
That is in you
Look straight ahead
To the finish line
Think only of the goal
Run straight
Run high
Run hard
Save nothing
And finish
With an ecstatic burst
That carries you
Hurtling
Through the tape
To victory...

FRANK HORNE
Afro-American

Me go u Granny Yard

Wha mek yu go Granny Yard?
  Me go Granny Yard
  fi go get sorrel drink.
And dat a really really true?
  Cahn yu hear a true?
Yu noh did go fi notn else?
  Dohn yu hear a notn else?

Wha mek yu go Granny Yard?
  Me go Granny Yard
  fi go get bwoil puddn.
An dat a really really true?
  Cahn yu hear a true?
Yu noh did go fi notn else?
  Dohn yu hear a notn else?

Wha mek yu go Granny Yard?
  Me go Granny Yard
  fi go get orange wine.
An dat a really really true?
  Cahn yu hear a true?
Yu noh did go fi notn else?
  Dohn yu hear a notn else?

Wha mek yu go Granny Yard?
  Me go Granny Yard
  fi go get cokenat cake.
An dat a really really true?
  Cahn yu hear a true?
Yu noh did go fi notn else?
  Dohn yu hear a notn else?

Wha mek yu go Granny Yard?
   Me go Granny Yard
   fi go get lemonade.
An dat a really really true?
   Cahn yu hear a true?
Yu noh did go fi notn else?
   Dohn yu hear a notn else?

Wha mek yu go Granny Yard?
   Me go Granny Yard
   fi go get ginger cookies.
An dat a really really true?
   Cahn yu hear a true?
Yu noh did go fi notn else
   Dohn yu hear a notn else?

Wha mek yu go Granny Yard?
   Me go Granny Yard
   fi go hide from punishment.
Fi go hide from punishment?
   Fi go hide from punishment!

JAMES BERRY
Jamaica/UK

113

A Proud Old Man (Grandpa)

They say they are healthier
   than me,
Though they can't walk to the
   end of a mile.
At their age I walked forty at night
   to wage battle at dawn.
They think they are healthier
   than me.
If their socks get wet they
   catch cold,
When my sockless feet got wet,
   I never sneezed,
But they still think that they are
   healthier than me.
On a soft mattress over a spring
   bed
They still have to take a sleeping
   pill.
But I, with reeds cutting into my
   ribs
My head resting on a piece of
   wood,
I sleep like a baby and snore.

PAUL CHIDYAUSIKU
Zimbabwe

Voice and Echoes

Voice

I am the voice that often speaks
I am the words that often weep
I am the choice of sounds you hear
I am the echo heard everywhere

We travel as one
And when you run
We're breathing in
And we're breathing out
To gain attention
We often shout.

Sometimes in your silent moods
You'll think of me
Before you decide
Before you choose

In the morning
When you sing and chant
Making the breakfast
When you know you can't.
I am the voice that never shouts
I am the voice you forget about.

I am the voice that often sings
I am the warmth beyond your lips
I am the rush of summer breeze
That lingers on like a floating breeze

When you wake
You will yawn
I am the long tone
That tells you
It is dawn.
I am the voice that often speaks
I am the voice that often weeps.

ALBIE OLLIVIERRE
*UK**

I Didn't Mean To

I didn't mean to laugh so loud
I made the windows rattle
and your jam jar split in two.
I didn't mean to laugh so loud
I made your best plates scatter
and your picture twisted on the wall.
I didn't mean to laugh so loud
your budgie flapped against the cage
and the television stopped.
I didn't mean to laugh so loud
the bulbs in your house just went POP.

Mummy always said that if I don't change my laugh
people will never invite me back to their house.

But when I grow up I'll change my name to
    THUNDER.

JOHN AGARD
Guyana/UK

118

My Song

Sitting, legs crossed, copper-toned old man
Chanting in low bass.
    'Ho aa Hey yah'
    'Way ah Hey ah'
Black Wolf is singing to the morning.
    'Hey aa ah Hey'
    'Way ah Hey aa'
He is singing to many years ago.
    'Hey ah Way Hey'
    'Way ah Hey aa'
The singing stops.
Drum silent.
Black Wolf looks down at his drum.
He has sung.

KING D. KUKA
American Indian (Blackfoot)

Questions I couldn't answer when asked by my four-year-old nephew...

I.   Why doesn't the river flow sidewise
     – bank to bank?

II. If 1 plus 1 is 2
     & 2 plus 2 makes 4
     how come 0 plus 0 is always zero?

III. What do the eyes of a bubble see?

IV. little daisies
     little lotuses
     little arches of rainbows
     &
     little birds
     little animals
     little oceans
     &
     little mountains
     &
     little people
     why didn't god make the world that way?

V.   Who is lonelier – the sun or the moon?

VI. If all of us talked in songs
     & not in words

     would we still be fighting?

VII. Why must everything die, Badbaba?

DEBA PATNAIK
India

A Poem About a Wolf Maybe Two Wolves

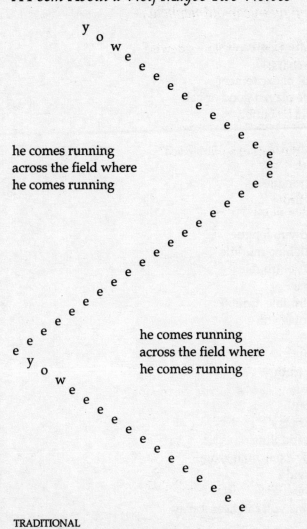

y
o
w
e
e
e
e
e
e
e
e
e
e
e
e
e
e
e
e

he comes running
across the field where
he comes running

e
e
e
e
e
e
e
e
e
e
e
e
e
e
e
e

he comes running
across the field where
he comes running

e
e
y
o
w
e
e
e
e
e
e
e
e
e
e
e
e
e
e
e
e
e

TRADITIONAL
North American Indian (Seneca)

De Tongue (De First Instrument)

De tongue
was de very first instrument
When it was played
it caused a lot of excitement
Now it can be played good or bad
de sounds can be bubbly
or be sad
It has been known
to tell de truth
den agen de tongue
can lie like a brute

If yuh lie wid yuh tongue
it will get yuh inna muddle
and you will get trouble
pon de double
Nuh bother trouble, trouble
weh nuh trouble yuh

I play I tongue
to project de truth
and hope I can
inspire de youths
I wish I could play
Drums, bass and flute
den I could be a one man group
But it sticks wid I
night and day
most of de time yuh can hear it play

BUM BUH BUM CHA, BUH BUH BUM BUM BAH CHA
BUM BUH BUM CHA, BUH BUH BUM BUM BAH CHA
BUM CHA BUM BUM BAH CHA
BUM CHA BUM BUM BAH CHA

It can be polite
and it can be rude
But what is unique
about dis instrument
is it can also taste FOOD

LEVI TAFARI
UK*

Speak

Speak – your lips are free
Speak – your tongue is still yours.
This magnificent body
Is still yours.
Speak – your life is still yours.
Look inside the smithy –
Leaping flames, red-hot iron.
Padlocks open wide
Their jaws.
Chains disintegrate.
Speak – there is little time
But little though it is
It is enough.
Time enough
Before the body perishes –
Before the tongue atrophies.
Speak – truth still lives.
Say what you have
To say.

FAIZ AHMAD FAIZ
Pakistan

She Tries Her Tongue... (Extract)

oath   moan   mutter   chant
     time grieves the dimension of other
babble   curse   chortle   sing
     turns on its axis of silence
praise-song   poem   ululation   utterance
     one song would bridge the finite in silence
syllable   vocable   vowel   consonant
     one word erect the infinite in memory

MARLENE NOURBESE PHILIP
Tobago and Trinidad

An Otomi Song of the Mexicans (Extract)

I, the singer, polished my noble new song like a shining
   emerald, arranged it like the voice of the *tzinitzcan* bird, I
   called to mind the essence of poetry, I set it in order like the
   chant of the *zacuan* bird, I mingled it with the beauty of the
   emerald, that I might make it appear like a rose bursting its
   bud, so that I might rejoice the Cause of All.

I skilfully arranged my song like the lovely feathers of the
   zacuan bird, the *tzinitzcan* and the *quechol*; I shall speak forth
   my song like the tinkling of golden bells; my song is that
   which the *miaua* bird pours forth around him; I lifted my
   voice and rained down flowers of speech before the face of
   the Cause of All.

In the true spirit of song I lifted my voice through a trumpet of
   gold, I let fall from my lips a celestial song, I shall speak
   notes precious and brilliant as those of the *miaua* bird, I shall
   cause to blossom out a noble new song, I lifted my voice like
   the burning incense of flowers, so that I the singer might
   cause joy before the face of the Cause of All.

Aztec Indian
Translated by Daniel Brinton

Wind Song

Wind now commences to sing;
   Wind now commences to sing.
The land stretches before me,
   Before me stretches away.

Wind's house now is thundering;
   Wind's house now is thundering.
I go roaring o'er the land,
   The land covered with thunder.

Over the windy mountains;
   Over the windy mountains,
Came the myriad-legged wind;
   The wind came running hither.

The Black Snake Wind came to me;
   The Black Snake Wind came to me,
Came and wrapped itself about,
   Came here running with its songs.

Pima Indian
Translated by Frank Russell

ECHOES   ECHOES

WHO AM I
WHO AM I

ECHOES   ECHOES
WHY AM I
WHY AM I

ECHOES   ECHOES
HOW DID I GET HERE
HOW DID I GET HERE

ABDUL MALIK
Trinidad

Telling It Like It Is

Baby-K Rap Rhyme

My name is Baby-K
An dis is my rhyme
Sit back folks
While I rap my mind;

Ah rocking with my homegirl,
My Mommy
Ah rocking with my homeboy,
My Daddy
My big sister, Les an
My Granny,
Hey dere people – my posse
I'm the business
The ruler of the nursery

poop po-doop
poop-poop po-doop
poop po-doop
poop-poop po-doop

Well, ah soaking up de rhythm
Ah drinking up my tea
Ah bouncing an ah rocking
On my Mommy knee
So happy man so happy

poop po-doop
poop-poop po-doop
poop po-doop
poop-poop po-doop

Wish my rhyme wasn't hard
Wish my rhyme wasn't rough
But sometimes, people
You got to be tough

Cause dey pumping up de chickens
Dey stumping down de trees
Dey messing up de ozones
Dey messing up de seas

Baby-K say, stop dis –
please, please, please

poop po-doop
poop-poop po-doop
poop po-doop
poop-poop po-doop

Now am splashing in de bath
With my rubber duck
Who don't like dis rhyme
Kiss my baby-foot
Babies everywhere
Join a Babyhood

Cause dey hotting up de globe, man
Dey hitting down de seals
Dey killing off de ellyies
For dere ivories
Baby-K say, stop dis –
please, please, please

poop po-doop
poop-poop po-doop
poop po-doop
poop-poop po-doop

Dis is my Baby-K rap
But it's a kinda plea
what kinda world
Dey going to leave fuh me?
What kinda world
Dey going to leave fuh me?
        Poop po-doop.

GRACE NICHOLS
Guyana/UK

Embarrassment

Being Indian
I'm easily embarrassed
Being Indian
I keep it in
Being Indian
I'm trained to

– and the techniques go back
five thousand years:

straight face, heartbeat steady,
not a muscle-twitch.

That's easy.

But the eyes –
ah those,
those are difficult...

I try.
I'm trained to.
I'm Indian.

PRABHU S. GUPTARA
India/UK

poem for ntombe iayo

(at five weeks of age)

who them people think
they are putting
me down here
on this floor

i'll just lay
here stretching
my arms and maybe i'll kick
my legs a li'l bit

why i betcha i'll just get up
from here and walk
soons i get big

NIKKI GIOVANNI
Afro-American

I am black as I thought
My lids are as brown as
I thought
My hair is curled as
I thought
I am free as I know

ACCABRE HUNTLEY
UK*

A Knowing Sister

I have a little babysister,
Who hasn't a care in the world,
She has jet black hair, fluffy and curled,
Her eyes are extremely bright and big
But when Kalera cries, you wonder,
Is it because she's hungry or tired?
Or is she aware, war shots are being fired?
And that the leaders of the world
Aren't that ozone friendly,
And the earth's protector is vanishing
Slowly but surely.
'What about my future?' Kalera seems to ask,
'Will we be just another memory gone in the past?'

LESLEY MIRANDA
UK

Corn and Potato

The corn and potato, peanut, strawberry:
Who gave them to us, can anyone tell me?
Canoes and snowshoes, hammocks for swinging:
Where did they come from in the beginning?

Was it Wonder Woman? No, No,
Six Million Dollar Man? No, No, No,
Was it Tom and Jerry? No, No,
Sylvester and Tweety? No, No, No,
Then was it Max B. Nimble? No, No,
Rocky and Bullwinkle? No, No, No,
Then was it Spiderman? No, No,
It must be Superman! No, No, No, No, No!

Next time you eat your strawberry jam
And peanuts, just ask your daddy this question,
Where did these come from: I'll give you one clue:
It wasn't Archie Bunker, that's all I can tell you.

Was it Paul Bunyan? No, No.
Was it Abraham Lincoln? No, No, No,.
Francisco Pizarro? No, No,
Was it Robinson Crusoe? No, No, No,
Was it a Pilgrim Father? No, No,
Or an old fur trader? No, No, No,
Columbus or Champlain? No, No,
Tennille and the Captain? No, No, No,
I give up, won't you tell me? Yes, Yes, Yes, Yes, Yes!

If you can't guess then I'd better tell you
Listen to me, I don't want to fool you
Before Columbus, before the Pilgrims,
These things and more all came from the Indians.

The Mic-Mac, the Sarcee, Yes, Yes,
Ojibway and Plains Cree, Yes, Yes, Yes,
The Sioux and the Cheyenne, Yes, Yes,
Apache and Peigan, Yes, Yes, Yes,
The Arawak or Taino, Yes, Yes,
The Mapuche, the Saulteaux, Yes, Yes, Yes,
The Hopi, the Haida, Yes, Yes,
The Inca, the Maya, Yes, Yes, Yes, Yes, Yes!
(I said Yes! Yes! Yes!)

DAVID CAMPBELL
Guyana

The Joy of Fishes

Chuang Tzu and Hui Tzu
Were crossing Hao river
By the dam.

Chuang said:
'See how free
The fishes leap and dart:
That is their happiness.'

Hui replied:
'Since you are not a fish
How do you know
What makes fishes happy?'

Chuang said:
'Since you are not I
How can you possibly know
That I do not know
What makes fishes happy?'

Hui argued:
'If I, not being you,
Cannot know what you know
It follows that you
Not being a fish
Cannot know what they know.'

Chuang said:
'Wait a minute!
Let us get back
To the original question.

What you asked me was
'How do you know
What makes fishes happy?'
From the terms of your question
You evidently know I know
What makes fishes happy.

'I know the joy of fishes
In the river
Through my own joy, as I go walking
Along the same river.'

CHUANG TZU
China
Translated by Thomas Merton

Airmail to a Dictionary

Black is...the shawl of the night
Secure from sharp paranoic light

Black is...the pupil of the eye
Putting colour in the sea's skin and earthen sky

Black is...the oil of the engine
On which this whole world is depending

Black is...light years of space
Holding on its little finger this human race

Black is...the colour of ink
That makes the history books we print

Black is...the colour of coal
Giving work to the miners, warmth to the old

Black is...the army. Wars in the night
Putting on the Black to hide the white

Black is...the strip on my cardcash
That lets me get money from the Halifax

Black is...the eclipse of the sun
displaying its power to every one

Black on Black is Black is Black
Strong as asphalt and tarmac

Black is...a word that I love to see.
Black is that, yeah, Black is me.

LEMN SISSAY
UK*

If You Have Time

If you have time to chatter
Read books

If you have time to read
Walk into mountain, desert and ocean

If you have time to walk
sing songs and dance

If you have time to dance
Sit quietly, you Happy Lucky Idiot.

NANAO SAKAKI
Japan

Can you?

Can you sell me the air as it slips through your fingers
As it slaps at your face and untidies your hair?
Perhaps you could sell me fivepennyworth of wind
or more, perhaps sell me a storm?
Perhaps the elegant air
you would sell me, that air
(not all of it) which trips around
your garden, from corolla to corolla
in your garden for the birds
tenpence worth of elegant air?

> The air spins and goes by
> in a butterfly.
> Belongs to no one, no one.

Can you sell me the sky
the sky sometimes blue
or grey as well sometimes
a strip of your sky
the bit you think you bought with the trees
of your garden, as one buys the roof with the house?
Can you sell me a dollar
of sky, two miles
of sky, a slice, whatever you can
of your sky?

> The sky is in the clouds
> The clouds go by
> Belong to no one, no one.

Can you sell me rain, the water
given you by your tears, and moistening your tongue?
Can you sell me a dollar of water
from a spring, a gravid cloud
crinkly and soft as a sheep
or perhaps rainwater up in the mountains
or the water from puddles
left for the dogs
or a stretch of sea, maybe a lake,
a hundred dollars of lake?

                    Water falls, rolls on.
                    Water rolls on, goes by.
                    Belongs to no one, no one.

Can you sell me the earth, the deep
night of the roots, teeth
of dinosaurs and the lime
dispersed from distant skeletons?
Can you sell me forests lying buried, birds that are dead
fishes of stone, the sulphur
of volcanoes, a thousand million years
twisting their way up? can you
sell me earth, can you
sell me earth, can you?

                    Your earth is mine.
                    Trodden by everyone's feet.
                    Belongs to no one, no one.

NICOLÁS GUILLÉN
Cuba

Index of First Lines

147

Index of Authors

Acknowledgements

The Publishers and the editor would like to thank the following for their kind permission to reprint copyright material in this book:

John Agard for 'I didn't mean to', 'The Clown's Wife', 'The Older the Violin', 'What the Teacher said', and 'Fisherman Chant'; Lillian Allen for 'Anancy' from *If you see the Truth* (Verse to Vinyl); Hamish Hamilton for 'A Toast for Everybody who is Growing' and 'Me go a Granny Yard' by James Berry from *When I Dance* by James Berry (Hamish Hamilton 1988, copyright © 1988 James Berry; Valerie Bloom for 'Water Everywhere' and 'Fruits'; William Stanley Braithwaite for 'Sea Lyric' from *Golden Slippers* ed. Arna Bontemps (Harper and Row); Dionne Brand for 'Hurricane' and 'Morning'; David Campbell for 'Corn and Potato' from *Man of Many Colours* (Elliot Chapin); Faustin Charles for 'Steelband Jump-up'; Debjani Chatterjee for 'Holding On' and 'Poem in the Post' from *I Was that Woman* (Hippopotamus Press); Afua Cooper for 'Kensington Market', 'It is Snowing' and 'Hopscotch'; GRM Associates, Inc., agents for the Estate of Ida M. Cullen for 'Under the Mistletoe' by Countee Cullen from the book *Copper Sun* by Countee Cullen, Copyright © 1927 by Harper & Brothers; Copyright renewed 1955 by Ida M. Cullen; Evans Brothers Ltd for 'Grandpa' by Paul Chidyansik from *African Voices* ed. H. Sergeant; Wesley Curtright for 'Heart of the Woods' from *Golden Slippers* (Harper and Row); Paul Dunbar for 'A Black Love Song' from *A Book of American Negro Poetry* (Harcourt Brace Jovanovich); David Durham for 'Daydreamer' from *You'll Love this Stuff* (Cambridge University Press); Nissim Ezekiel for 'For Kalpana' from *An Anthology of Indo-English Poetry* (Hind Pocket Books, Delhi); Faiz Ahmad Faiz for 'Speak' from *One for Blair*; Lynford French for 'Me in the Morning' (Black Ink Collective); Zulfikar Ghose for 'The Picnic in Jammu'; Nikki Giovanni for 'Two Friends' and 'Poem for Ntombe Iayo' (Hill and Wang) and Random House Inc. for 'The Reason I Like Chocolate' by Nikki Giovanni from *The Walker Book of Poetry*; Grace Gordon for 'Roots Man'; Harper and Row for 'Honey I Love' and 'Fun' by Eloise Greenfield from *Honey I Love*; the University of Nebraska Press for 'An Otomi Song of the Mexicans' and 'Wind Song' from *The Sky Clears* by A. Grove Day; 'Can You?' by Nicolás Guillén from *The Great Zoo* (Instituto Cubano del Libro); Ranjeet Guptara for 'Boring Chores' and 'The Literary Cat';

Prabhu Guptara for 'In Praise of Noses' and 'Embarrassment'; Geetanjali Guptara for 'Imagining India'; Frank Horne for 'To James' from *Golden Slippers* ed. Arna Bontemps (Harper and Row); Harold Ober Associates, New York for 'Sailor' and 'April Rain Song' by Langston Hughes from *The Dream Keeper and other Poems*; Accabre Huntley for 'I am Black'; Eva Johnson for 'Weevilly Porridge' from *Inside Black Australia* (Penguin Australia); Terry Kee for 'Grown-Up Blues' from *Sincerely Yours* (Tate Publishing, Singapore); Miriam Khamadi for 'They Ran out of Mud' from *Rhymes and Rhythms* (Oxford University Press); King Kuka for 'My Song' from *Voices of the Rainbow* ed. Kenneth Rosen (The Press Inc., New York); Charlotte Steedy Literary Agency, New York for 'Hanging Fire' by Audre Lorde from *The Black Unicorn*; Penguin Books Ltd for 'Teasing Song' by Princess Magogo, from *The Penguin Book of Oral Poetry* ed. Ruth Finnegan, copyright © 1978 Ruth Finnegan; The Panrun Collective for 'Echoes' by Abdul Malik; Harrivakore Maripo for 'Rain O Rain O' from *Words of Paradise* ed. Ulli Beier (Unicorn Press, California); Frank Marshall Davis for 'Rain' from *Golden Slippers* ed. Arna Bontemps (Harper and Row); Marc Matthews for 'When'; University of Nebraska Press for 'First Song of Thunder' trans. Dr Matthews from *The Sky Clears*; Wong May for 'Only the Moon; Lesley Miranda for 'A Knowing Sister' and 'Miss Pinn'; Stella Miria for 'I Built a Canoe' from *Words of Paradise* ed. Ulli Beier (Unicorn Press, California); Michael Mondo for 'Sun and Shade' from *Words of Paradise* ed. Ulli Beier (Unicorn Press, California); Pamela Mordecai for 'What to Do'; Open Hand Publishing (Seattle) for 'Mamacita' and 'Night in the Lap of Morning' from *Nightfeathers* by Sundaira Morninghouse; the University of Iowa Press for 'My Baby has no name yet' by Kim Nam-Jo from *Contemporary Korean Poetry*; Penguin Books (Australia) for 'The Two Mothers' by Rhonda Napurrurla from *Inside Black Australia*; Penguin Books (Australia) for 'The Kangaroo' by Pansy Napaljarri from *Inside Black Australia*; University of Nebraska Press for 'Song of the Horse' trans. Curtis Natalie from *Song of the Thunder*; Grace Nichols for 'My Cousin Melda' and 'Granny Granny Please Comb My Hair'; Viking Children's Books for 'Baby-K Rap Rhyme' by Grace Nichols from *No Hickory, No Dickory, No Dock* by Grace Nichols and John Agard (Viking, 1991); Paladin Books for 'Voice' by Albie Ollivierre from *New British Poetry*; P. Omoboye for 'I know the answer' from *The Bees Knees* ed.

155

Gary Boswell (Stride Press); Opal Palmer Adisa for 'De More de Merrier' and 'I Wonder'; Deba Patnaik for 'Questions I Couldn't Answer' from *You'll Love this Stuff* (Cambridge University Press); Marlene Philip for the extract from 'She Tries Her Tongue...'; Bantam Doubleday Inc for 'Ballad of Birmingham' by Dudley Randall from *The Black Poets*; Alfred van der Marck Editions for 'A Poem about a Wolf maybe Two Wolves' from *Shaking the Pumpkin*; Tooth of Time Books (New Mexico) for 'If you have time' by Nanao Sakaki from *Poetry and Drama*; Lemn Sissay for 'Airmail to a Dictionary' from *The Bees Knees* (Stride Publishing); Precedent Publishing (Chicago) for 'Timing' by Elma Stuckey from *The Big Gate*; Mambo Press for 'To you Ant' from *Mambo Book of Zimbabwean Verse*; Levi Tafari for 'De Tongue'; Thomas Nelson & Sons for 'I Wish I Were' by Rabindranath Tagore; Random House Inc. for 'My Kind of School' by Raymond Teeseteskie from *Belly of the Shark*; Odette Thomas for 'Confusion'; Telcine Turner for 'Morning Break'; Laurence Pollinger for 'The Joy of Fishes' by Chuang Tzu trans. Thomas Merton from *The Way of Chuang Tzu* (New Directions Publishing Corporation); Centerprise Publishing for 'My Name is I Don't Know' by Vivian Usherwood from *Poems*; Oxford University Press (Nairobi) for 'A Comb' by Gautam Vohra from *Zuak 6 Journal*' George Allen & Unwin for 'Blaming Sons' and 'The Lychee' trans. Arthur Waley from *170 Chinese Poems*.

Every effort has been made to trace copyright holders but the editor and Publisher apologise if any inadvertent omission has been made.